PERFORMANCE EDITIONS

LABORUM DULCE LENIMEN

G. SCHIRMER

MENDELSSOHN

SELECTIONS FROM SONGS WITHOUT WORDS

T0080181

Edited and Recorded by Immanuela Gruenberg

AUDIO ACCESS INCLUDED
Recorded Performances Online

To access companion recorded performances online, visit:
www.halleonard.com/mylibrary

Enter Code
7257-9828-2351-8810

On the cover:
View of Florence (1830)
by Felix Mendelssohn (1809–1847)

ISBN 978-1-4803-6027-3

G. SCHIRMER, Inc.

DISTRIBUTED BY
HAL•LEONARD®
CORPORATION
7777 W. BLUEMOUND RD. P.O. BOX 13819 MILWAUKEE, WI 53213

Copyright © 2014 by G. Schirmer, Inc. (ASCAP) New York, NY
International Copyright Secured. All Rights Reserved.

**Warning: Unauthorized reproduction of this publication is
prohibited by Federal law and subject to criminal prosecution.**

www.musicsalesclassical.com
www.halleonard.com

CONTENTS

The price of this publication includes access to companion recorded performances online, for download or streaming, using the unique code found on the title page. Visit **www.halleonard.com/mylibrary** and enter the access code.

HISTORICAL NOTES

FELIX MENDELSSOHN (1809–1847)

Felix Mendelssohn was raised in a bourgeois aristocratic household in Berlin. His parents, Abraham Mendelssohn and Lea Itzig, came from prominent families afforded special governmental privileges not available to most Prussian Jews. Their home was frequented by leading artists, musicians, writers, and thinkers such as Heinrich Heine, Friedrich Hegel, and Alexander von Humboldt. In 1816, Felix and his siblings were baptized as Protestants, and when his parents converted to Protestantism several years later the family took on the new surname Bartholdy. Felix's mother Lea and her sisters were talented pianists, music collectors, and salonnières. Both Lea and her sister Sarah received piano lessons from students of J.S. Bach. Sarah amassed a large collection of scores by J.S. and C.P.E. Bach, to whom she was a devoted patron. This love of Bach was passed on to Felix, who played an important role in the Bach revival; he is credited with expanding J.S. Bach's appeal beyond the intellectual elite with his organization of a performance of the *St. Matthew Passion* at the Singakademie in Berlin in 1829.

"Felix Mendelssohn Bartholdy" by Eduard Magnus - Staatsbibliothek Preussischer Kulturbesitz, Berliner

Mendelssohn was a preeminent composer, conductor, organist, and pianist during his lifetime. As a composer he excelled in a multitude of genres, including the symphony, string quartet, and oratorio. The overture to *A Midsummer Night's Dream* was well received upon its premiere in 1827 and remains one of his most beloved works. The unique texture of the light and spritely opening has come to be known as a "fairy" scherzo. The style is found in other works as well, including the scherzo movement of his wonderful String Octet, Op. 20.

Felix and his older sister Fanny were child prodigies and both received the same stellar musical education. This included piano lessons with Ludwig Berger in Berlin and Marie Bigot in Paris, as well as theory and composition instruction from Carl Friedrich Zelter, director of the Singakademie. Mendelssohn's parents likely chose Zelter to instruct their children due to his conservative tastes. His lessons included careful study

of scores by Bach, Mozart, and Haydn. Felix's early compositions reflect the tenor of his education, but following the end of his studies with Zelter in 1824 inspiration from more contemporary composers such as Beethoven and Weber began seeping into his works.

Mendelssohn composed piano music throughout his career. The biggest influences in his keyboard writing were drawn from J.S. Bach's contrapuntal techniques, the emotional power of Beethoven's middle and late periods, and the light textures of Weber. Although Mendelssohn was a great pianist, he did not test the limits of piano technique like Liszt or Chopin. Mendelssohn did not use composition as a means towards sparkling displays of virtuosity, but had instead other priorities. His piano compositions include sonatas, fantasies, character pieces, preludes and fugues, and theme and variations. Mendelssohn's *Songs Without Words (Lieder ohne Worte)*, however, marked the creation of an entirely new genre. His first such work was composed for Fanny's birthday in 1828.[1] Fanny composed a number of pieces in the genre as well, and it may have its roots in a game the two played, in which they put words to especially lyrical piano works.[2] The siblings' close relationship, made extraordinary through their shared passion and talent for music, is well documented in correspondence and personal diaries. The *Songs Without Words* provide one example of how Fanny's talents stimulated Felix's compositional imagination through play and conversation.

Mendelssohn's death from a series of strokes at age 38 in 1847 was mourned as a severe blow to Europe's musical establishment. *The Musical World* referred to his death as the "eclipse of music."[3] Later in the Romantic era, however, Mendelssohn's music fell out of favor in Germany. There was little room for Mendelssohn in the growing understanding of German art music as a teleological progression from Bach to Mozart to Beethoven to Wagner. Wagner himself helped to propagate this attitude in his writings, most notably his virulently anti-Semitic essay *Judaism in Music*. During the Third Reich, the Nazis banned Mendelssohn's music and removed his statue from the front of the Leipzig Conservatory. Post-World War II, Mendelssohn's status among the great composers of the nineteenth century rose again. Interest in his works has increased as previously unpublished pieces have become available to the public. The availability of primary source material, including Mendelssohn's manuscripts, diaries, paintings and letters, has inspired Mendelssohn scholarship that continues to boost appreciation and understanding of his works and the important role his family played in the intellectual and artistic life of eighteenth and nineteenth century Germany.

—*Rachel Kelly*

[1] Fanny was a child prodigy and great musical talent, but her position as a female in a family of bourgeois aristocrats kept her from a public career enjoyed by female contemporaries such as Clara Schumann. For more on this topic, see: Nancy Reich, "The Power of Class: Fanny Hensel and the Mendelssohn Family" in *Women's Voices Across Musical Worlds*, ed. Jane A. Bernstein (Boston: Northeastern University Press, 2004).

[2] R. Larry Todd, "Mendelssohn, Felix," *Grove Music Online, Oxford Music Online*, Oxford University Press, accessed August 5, 2014, http://www.oxfordmusiconline.com/subscriber/article/grove/music/51795pg14.

[3] Ibid., accessed July 31, 2014.

PERFORMANCE NOTES

"[Words] ...seem so ambiguous, so vague, so subject to misunderstanding when compared with true music, which fills the soul with a thousand better things than words."[1] —Felix Mendelssohn

Exquisitely beautiful and wonderfully imaginative, Mendelssohn's *Songs Without Words* are also practical from a pianistic point of view. A virtuoso pianist himself, Mendelssohn incorporated the piano's various sonorities and the instrument's wide range of technical possibilities into these short works.

There are eight volumes of six songs each, and it appears that no two of the forty-eight songs are alike—a testament to the inspiration and originality of Mendelssohn's creative mind. The first six books were published during Mendelssohn's lifetime; the last two consist of works selected posthumously by publishers eager to produce additional publications of this highly popular genre.

The present publication contains fifteen *Songs Without Words*. In playing through all these beautiful gems, I found that one of the hardest tasks was deciding which of the original forty-eight to leave out as each seemed to beckon to me to be included. The fifteen works selected include at least one representative from each of the eight opuses, works of different technical levels (including several of the easier ones) and of a wide variety of moods, characters, tempos, and musical and technical elements. They appear here in chronological order.

Through these works, pianists and students can learn and improve many musical aspects, including
- voicing
- shaping of melodic lines
- "layering" and polyphonic playing
- control of a wide dynamic range
- articulation
- making the piano sing
- transferring lines between the two hands

and various technical issues such as
- repeated notes
- chords
- octaves
- leaps
- staccato
- *leggiero*
- fast runs

and so on.

Style and Interpretation
Mendelssohn's Style

Mendelssohn was at once conservative and ahead of his time. Influenced by his main teacher Carl Friedrich Zelter, he admired and carefully studied and researched the music of Bach, Handel, Mozart, and Beethoven. In the preface to the 1915 edition for Schirmer's Library of Musical Classics, Constantin von Sternberg, the editor, writes that classifying Mendelssohn as a Romantic composer

> ...is not altogether just, inasmuch as it applies to one side only in the wide compass of his musical personality, and not even to its strongest side, for it emphasizes unduly that romanticism which was only an incidental feature in his manysided genius. The classification is somewhat unjust to Mendelssohn's other and far more pronounced characteristics; especially to those which so markedly differentiate him from his great contemporaries and which entitle him to be regarded as a "Classic-Romantic"—in fact, *the* Classic-Romantic.[2]

Hans von Bülow said the following:

> In Mendelssohn, you do not need to interpret; he wrote everything scrupulously and exactly as he wanted to have it. The master shows himself by his restraint; he does not try to do more than he is able to accomplish...[3]

Early nineteenth-century concerts were often devoted to the performance of new, contemporary compositions. The historical concerts and festivals that Mendelssohn organized and conducted played a key role in changing that, acquainting the concert-going public with the music of the older masters and setting the tone for the classical concert as we know it today. At age twenty, Mendelssohn conducted the first performance in nearly a century of Bach's *St. Matthew's Passion*. This concert, which was a great success, was the turning point that led to the revival of Bach's music. At the same time, Mendelssohn was also regularly promoting and performing the music of his contemporaries.

Mendelssohn's great regard for the music of the old masters is clearly evident in his own music, including the *Songs Without Words*. The use of polyphony, chorale-like writing, clear articulation between and within phrases, clear and transparent textures, and refinement and expressive restraint, all point to influences by Bach, Handel, and Mozart. Mendelssohn nevertheless took full advantage of the more extensive colors and wider dynamic range of the nineteenth-century pianoforte. In fact, the very idea of *Songs Without Words* is based on merging the Romantic miniature with the German art song of that same period while utilizing the pianoforte's new sonorities.

As editor, Mendelssohn took the unusual (at the time) approach of including no markings besides those of the composer, a practice that became the norm only in the second half of the twentieth century.

Contrary to contemporary composers such as Schumann and Berlioz, Mendelssohn did not write program or autobiographical music (although, as we shall see in regard to two of the songs, his music *did* reflect his personal life). When his music isn't abstract, it is descriptive, evoking certain moods, feelings, or images. While literary works did influence some of his compositions, most of Mendelssohn's music, including the *Songs Without Words*, does not follow a storyline or a plot. It sometimes paints a picture or describes a scene, a landscape, or a mood, setting to music Mendelssohn's strong visual perceptions and gifts as a painter. In a letter to the Leipzig music publisher Friedrich Kistner, dated January 3, 1835, Mendelssohn wrote "I am in no way in a position to speak on music properly for even a half hour, let alone throughout an entire colloquium..." and that on such occasions "[I] always came away feeling more unmusical than I did when I went in..."[4] This quote demonstrates Mendelssohn's feeling that music was very clear and comprehensible to him, while words seemed ambiguous. From here, a logical outcome are "Songs Without Words," compositions in which music, and music alone, says all he has to say and all he wants to express.

Mendelssohn as Performer

A virtuoso yet sensitive pianist, a world-class conductor, an extraordinary improviser, and a gifted violinist and organist, Mendelssohn, according to accounts by those who knew him personally and heard him perform, was a serious, conscientious performer who meticulously followed the score, preferred fast, vigorous tempos, and opposed sentimentality and affectation.[5] Performers of Mendelssohn's music would do well to heed these accounts.

Charles Edward Horsley, who met Mendelssohn in London, studied with him and heard him perform, wrote the following:

> I do not however think that full justice has yet been done to his marvelous powers as an executive musician. As an Organ and Pianoforte player he has never been excelled. His playing of the Organ has been already mentioned, but his management of the Piano was if possible still more marvelous. His powers of execution were quite as great as those of [Anton] Rubinstein and Liszt; his delicacy of touch and tone was not exceeded by Thalberg or Chopin; and when all these qualities are added the wonderful scope of his own mind in grasping the Pianoforte music of all schools, I do not in the least exaggerate when I assert that, of all pianoforte players of and since his time, Mendelssohn stands by far on the apex of greatness.[6]

His early biographer W. A. Lampadius wrote the following:

> Mendelssohn's skill...was that true, manly *virtus* from which the word virtuoso is derived; that steadfast energy which overcomes all mechanical hindrances, not to produce musical noise, but music... The characteristic features of his playing were a very elastic touch, a wonderful trill, elegance, roundness, firmness, perfect articulation, strength, and tenderness, each in its needed place. His chief excellence lay, as Goethe said, in his giving every piece, from the Bach epoch down, its own distinctive character.[7]

Schumann, upon hearing Mendelssohn perform his second piano concerto, wrote: "I often think that Mozart must have played like that." In a similar vein, Hans von Bülow recommended pianists play Mozart before playing Mendelssohn and abstain from sentimentality and pomposity when performing Mendelssohn's music.

Mendelssohn and the Piano

Mendelssohn's piano teachers included Marie Bigot who was a friend of, and admired by, Haydn and Beethoven; Ludwig (Louis) Berger, his principal teacher (and student of Clementi),[8] Ignaz Moscheles,[9] and Hummel.[10]

According to R. Larry Todd, "[w]hether composing for the piano or other media, Mendelssohn habitually used in his sketches a two-stave, treble-bass format, suggesting that if he did not work at the piano, the sound of the instrument was never far removed from the wellspring of his imagination."[11] And Hans von Bülow said that Mendelssohn "...writes for the piano in a manner suitable for the piano..."[12]

From the time he was seven Mendelssohn owned a Broadwood fortepiano. Later, he also had an Erard fortepiano and a Silbermann clavichord. He also played the harpsichord. On his many travels, he tried out various instruments by English, French, German, and Austrian makers. [13] These fortepianos had a lighter touch, a softer tone, and a shallower key-fall than the modern piano, allowing for easier, more effortless playing. Even by these standards, Mendelssohn's playing stood out as being "extremely subtle, and developed with the lightest of wrists (never from the arm); he therefore never strained the instrument or hammer. His chord-playing was beautiful ... his phrasing beautifully clear." [14]

Pedal

"His use of the pedal was very scant, clearly defined, and therefore effective;" [15]

All pedal markings in this edition are by the composer. A number of things become evident when looking at these markings. These markings are indeed, scant (Op. 19, No. 2; Op. 30, No. 3; Op. 62, No. 3). Pedal changes are indicated primarily when the bass or harmony change, and not necessarily when the top line has stepwise motion (Op. 19, No. 3, mm. 12–15 and 18–23; Op. 19, No. 6, mm. 34–40; Op. 30, No. 6, mm. 39–41). Mendelssohn often indicates lengthy pedals at endings of pieces (Op. 19, No. 3; Op. 30, No. 6; Op. 53, No. 3; Op. 62, No. 3). The so-called "Spring Song," Op. 62, No. 6 in A Major, offers an interesting example of Mendelssohn's use of pedal for special effects, or special sonorities. These are general comments. For specifics, see the discussions of each piece below.

Tempo

As noted above, Mendelssohn seems to have favored brisk tempos both when playing and when conducting, and opposed *ritardandos* not indicated in the score. Clara Schumann said that "[h]e would sometimes take the tempi very quick, but never to the prejudice of the music." [16] An article that appeared in 1841 in the Philadelphia *National Gazette* has, among other things, this to say about Mendelssohn's playing: "expression ... requiring not the garnishing of trills and *appogiaturas, or the aid of changes of time* [emphasis added], are among its outward and salient characteristics." [17] That said, we must remember that the style of his playing was regarded and commented on in comparison to his contemporaries, at least some of whom favored extensive *rubatos* and adding their own "personal touches." In a letter to his family, Mendelssohn—his high regard for Liszt notwithstanding—offers a highly critical account of how the latter tampered with the music of Bach, Beethoven, Handel, and Weber at a concert he performed:

Here six measures added in, there seven omitted; here he plays false harmonies, and then later these are cancelled out by others. Then he makes a horrible fortissimo out of the softest passages, and goodness knows what other kinds of dreadful mischief. [18]

Songs Without Words

"A Mendelssohn Song Without Words is as Classical to me as a Goethe poem." [19] —Hans von Bülow

The exact origin of this oxymoronic title is not known but the title helps to illustrate Mendelssohn's conviction that music—absolute, abstract music—is more meaningful and more precise than words. The first known reference to this title dates from November 1828 when Mendelssohn sent to his sister Fanny a birthday present of a piano piece entitled *Lied*, or Song. Later, Fanny referred to this composition as a *Lied ohne Worte*, or Song Without Words.

Six of the eight volumes of *Lieder ohne Worte* were published between 1832 and 1845, during Mendelssohn's lifetime. These are opus numbers 19, 30, 38, 53, 62, and 67. The last two volumes, opus numbers 85 and 102, are compilations of short pieces from Mendelssohn's estate, assembled and published posthumously. The first opus was published in England in 1832 as *Original Melodies for the Pianoforte* and in France as 6 *Romances sans paroles*. But it was *Lieder ohne Worte* that became the popular, enduring title.

Success was not immediate, but once it came, it was enormous. Musicians and amateurs alike loved the songs, and many composers imitated their style. In the preface to his Bärenreiter edition, R. Larry Todd lists the following compositions as containing *Lieder ohne Worte*-inspired instances: Schumann's *Fantasiestücke*, Op. 12; Liszt's Petrarch Sonnets; Brahms' slow movements of his piano sonatas; compositions by Louis Spohr, Stephen Heller, Henry Litolff, Charles Gounod, George Bizet, Tchaikovsky, and Richard Strauss, all of whom used that title. In addition, Charles Ives wrote a "Song without (good) Words" and Schönberg wrote a *Lied (ohne Worte)*. Even though they are intimate in nature and were probably conceived with the intention of being played in relatively private settings (Mendelssohn himself often played them to his friends and family), the songs have been studied, and performed in public by many of the greatest pianists, beginning with Mendelssohn's contemporaries Sigismond Thalberg and Hans von Bülow all the way to the present. When Ferruccio Busoni died in 1924, an open copy of the *Songs Without Words* was found on his piano. In my own research for this publication, I found a publication of the songs edited by Maurice Ravel.

The great success and popularity these compositions enjoyed led to the creation of many nicknames and titles, but only six of the forty-eight songs were given titles by the composer himself: three Venetian Boat Songs (*Gondellieder*), Op. 19b, No. 6, Op. 30, No. 6, and Op. 62 No. 5; *Duet*, Op. 38, No. 6; Folk song (*Volkslied*), Op. 53, No. 5; and Children's Piece (*Kinderstück*), Op. 102, No. 3. In his correspondences, Mendelssohn often referred to Op. 62, No. 6 as *Frühlingslied*, or Spring Song, but did not include the title in the publication.

In many of the *Lieder ohne Worte*, the main musical idea appears several times, each time with only minor changes in either the melody or the accompaniment. Such subtleties are to be expected from a composer who shunned exaggeration of any kind. They require great attention to detail as well as restraint.

Sources

Mendelssohn was meticulous in his writing and editing. He was also highly self-critical, often repeatedly sending changes and corrections to publishers. Therefore, many different sources of the *Songs Without Words* exist, though not all sources of each song survive. Existing sources include the composer's manuscripts (sometimes more than one version) and early editions. Renewed interest in Mendelssohn over the past thirty-some years has brought about new scholarly editions of his works. For this publication, I have consulted the following editions: G. Henle Verlag, edited by Rudolf Elvers and Ernst Herttrich (1981); Wiener Urtext, edited by Christa Jost (2001); Bärenreiter, edited by R. Larry Todd (2009); G. Schirmer, edited by Constantin von Sternberg (1915); Breitkopf and Härtel, edited by Julius Rietz (1874–1877). Since opus numbers 85 and 102 were published after Mendelssohn's death, he did not oversee their publication, so we cannot be sure whether he would have authorized the versions we now consider definitive.

Notes on the Individual Works
Song Without Words in A minor, Op. 19b, No. 2

The clear, transparent texture of this Song Without Words is reminiscent of Mozart's textures. This is mainly a solo-melody song, but contains instances of duets, as in measures 3–8. It also contains a contrapuntal, slightly hidden line within the sixteenth-note accompaniment. Although the texture, polyphony, and short slurs seem more in line with Baroque or Classical than with Romantic style, Mendelssohn manages to create a romantic expression with means borrowed from older styles.

The counterpoint, like the main voice, needs to be carefully shaped. Make sure not to emphasize the left hand's back-and-forth, oscillating motion but focus instead on the horizontal line. It is important to pay attention to the clearly-marked articulation signs and to the various touches the composer indicates (accents, *sforzandos*, wedges, *portato*). Also note that while there are numerous dynamic markings, the range is mostly *mf* to *pp*. *f* is reached only once, in measure 38. Overall, this piece should sound intimate and delicate.

Song Without Words in A Major, Op. 19b, No. 3

Marked *Molto Allegro e vivace*, this is a lively, energetic, bravura piece. Often referred to by editors as a Hunting Song, it brings to mind horn calls and the thrill of a chase. The thrill, excitement, and momentum should be maintained throughout in loud, as well as in soft passages. The melody is a multi-part homophonic song. It calls for strong fingers and voicing of the chords in both the right and the left hand. Rhythmically marked, this piece should be played with a great deal of rhythmic control while also maintaining, throughout, a forward motion. Momentum is all the more important when playing repeated chords and repeated octaves in order to keep them from sounding like stepping in place.

Pay special attention to the pedal. Several of Mendelssohn's markings may create a blurry sound on some of today's pianos. Depending on the particular piano and specific acoustics, it may at times be necessary to release the pedal half way (for example, on the second beat in measures 18, 20, etc.; between measures 51–54, 57–60, and so on) in order to avoid dissonances while keeping the bass in the pedal.

Song Without Words in G minor "Venetian Boat Song," Op. 19b, No. 6

This is the first of the three highly popular Venetian Boat Songs. (In addition to the three Boat Songs, or *Gondellieder*, that are part of the forty eight *Songs Without Words*, there is another Boat Song in A Major that Mendelssohn composed in 1841). Compositions in this genre, otherwise known as Barcarolles (barca means boat in Italian), are in 6/8 or 12/8 meter, moving in a gently flowing pace that evokes a boat swaying smoothly on the lapping waters of a canal in Venice. Some of the most famous Barcarolles are Chopin's Barcarolle, Op. 60, in F-sharp Major and the Barcarolle from Offenbach's opera *The Tales of Hoffmann*. As a matter of fact, in the 1832 English First Edition, this particular Song Without Words was called Barcarolle.[20] This song's melodic line is a duet in parallel thirds or parallel sixths, moving above bass notes and a middle layer of broken chords.

The nature of the sound that is created in measures 1–6, where the accompaniment is divided between the two hands, should be maintained throughout the piece, even when that same material is played by the left hand alone. In measures 22–23, the long pedal, the diminished-seventh harmony, and the *pianissimo* dynamic all work together to create a special color effect. In measures 34–40 however, you may want to use half pedal or flutter pedal in order to follow Mendelssohn's indications of a long, sustained pedal over the pedal point G, while making sure not to create too blurry a sound. Bringing out the bass-note G while playing the rest of the harmony softer can also help. In measures 19–20 pay special attention to the left-hand articulation versus the right-hand *legato* that leads from G to the accented A-flat on the second beat. The right-hand articulation changes in measure 22 and again in measure 23 where the third eighth A is transformed from a melody note (m. 22) to an accompaniment note (m. 23).

Song Without Words in E Major, Op. 30, No. 3

The subtle way in which Mendelssohn varies this multi-voice, chorale-like Song Without Words is characteristic of his often understated style. Compare, for example, the second half of measure 3 to the corresponding part in measure 17; measure 6 to measure 10, and measure 20 to measure 24. Also compare the dynamics in measures 4–5 to measures 9–10 and 19–20.

As pianists, we are trained to voice chords and to "bring out the melody." But occasionally we should opt for a sound that is more harmony than melody, more choir than solo voice. This Song Without Words offers the opportunity to voice when the music calls for it, as in measures 3, 4, and the first half of measure 5, and not to voice when the writing is homophonic, as it is in measures 5 (second half) to measure 6 (first chord), measures 11–14, etc. This alteration between soloist and choir adds a spiritual dimension to the piece by invoking liturgical elements.

Although it is one of the easier *Songs Without Words* from a purely technical standpoint, this song poses a number of artistic challenges. The 4/4 meter means that the *Adagio non troppo* applies to the quarter note, not the eighth. The danger of this piece becoming too slow and static is further exacerbated by chordal motion that emphasizes verticality. Make sure to always have a sense of the horizontal line and the forward motion. Pay special attention to Mendelssohn's articulation and to the different touches he indicates. Also notice the difference between a syncopated two-note slur (B–A in mm. 4, 18) where the second note,

while softer than the first, has to maintain its sound, and a non-syncopated one (G-sharp–F-sharp in m. 5, and B–A-sharp in m. 13), where the second note is shorter and softer than the first one.

Song Without Words in F-sharp minor "Venetian Boat Song," Op. 30, No. 6

Marked *Allegretto tranquillo*, this Song Without Words has a flowing accompaniment and very expressive melodic line. This song moves at a faster pace than the Boat Song in G minor, Op. 19, No. 6, and has a more open, less subdued feel. The first hint of a melody—in double thirds, as a duet—is introduced as part of the accompaniment in measures 5–6 and the melodic line itself seems to emerge from this part of the accompaniment. After the double bar, the duet that was only hinted at in measures 5–6 takes center stage, reinforcing the two elements that make up both the melody and accompaniment: single-note lines and double thirds.

Pay special attention to instances of repeated notes, measures 7–9, 15–17, and 37–39. The risk is that the five successive C-sharps sound too similar, creating stasis. Take into account the carefully placed hairpins that denote a slight crescendo to the high A—an expressive means that follows the contour of the melodic line but is at odds with the meter, making it more striking.

See also the discussion of Venetian Boat Song, Op. 19b, No 6, above.

Song Without Words in A-flat Major "Duet," Op. 38, No 6

One of the few *Songs Without Words* to be given a title by Mendelssohn himself, the *Duet* also bears the following note by the composer: "Both voices must always be brought out clearly" ("*N. B. Die beiden Stimmen müssen immer sehr deutlich hervorgehoben werden*"). Along with the title, this comment underscores this song's distinctive quality: it is for two equally important and independent voices rather than the customary one, and unlike a standard duet, the two voices are not moving in parallel thirds or sixths. This comment may have been necessary because in some of the songs, the accompanying line does sound more melodic and more significant than "mere" accompaniment, but should not be assumed to be as important as the main melody. Case in point: Op. 19b, No. 1, Op. 38, No 2, (not included in this publication) Op. 67, No. 3, and Op. 85, No. 2 (see below). The tempo, *Andante con moto* and the 6/8 meter, indicate that this song should not be played too slowly, as some are tempted to do.

Composed in 1836 during Mendelssohn's engagement to Cecile Jeanrenaud who was to become his wife, this song illustrates a dialogue between male and female voices. The conversation starts with the high (female) voice singing a four-bar melody (A), to which the low (male) voice replies (mm. 6–9) with melody B. The high voice restates its melody (A), this time with slightly different, more interesting, more tender harmonies, to which the low voice replies with melody B, this time in the dominant E-flat. Up to this point, each of the two melodies is four measures long. Measure 18 introduces a new, one-measure long melody (C) in the high voice to which the low voice replies with a one-measure fragment of its own melody (B). The dialogue's intensity increases, with the tenor and soprano interacting in a sort of *stretto* (mm. 30–31) that turns to homophony (mm. 32–39) in a melody that is based primarily on B but includes motivic elements from A.

This song consists of a total of four layers. In addition to the soprano and tenor—the two singing voices—a bass line that itself is melodic on occasion, and an arabesque-like accompaniment of sixteenth-note triplets. Each of these layers has its own place in the piece, its distinctive character, and its own function, and should therefore have its unique color and touch.

In a number of instances, the middle layer(s) can be played by either hand. The fingering and hand distributions I have found most helpful are indicated in the score but you are encouraged to experiment in order to find what works best for your own hands and ears. In measures 45–47 the right hand plays three different, distinctive voices simultaneously without the possibility of the left hand helping out. Their proximity adds to the difficulty of aurally distinguishing between them. Make an effort to show there are three voices. The *f* drama that began in measure 32 fades away gradually and gives way to a calm *p* where, in the last measure, when all is peaceful and quiet, only two notes, reminders of the two main voices, live on.

Song Without Words in E-flat Major, Op. 53, No. 2

Several things make this beautiful and expressive *Song Without Words* difficult and tricky to pull off. A deeply expressive, duple-rhythm meter is accompanied by animated, repeated chords in triplets. Bringing out the single-line melody against the thick-textured accompaniment is a challenge and requires that the full, dense chords be played softly enough to allow the thinner melody to shine through. Mendelssohn's pedal markings are very clear: pedal on the long notes, no pedal during the melody's stepwise

movement. This, however, creates its own challenge because the result is a sudden change in tone and color where continuity, not change, is called for. This kind of pedaling may not have been a problem on Mendelssohn's pianos mainly because the pianoforte's dampers were slower at muting the sound, thus the release of the pedal did not create a sudden, abrupt change. When playing this song on the modern piano, the remedy may be half or flutter pedal, requiring constant, careful listening.

Song Without Words in G minor, Op. 53, No. 3

This is one of the most energetic and exciting of the *Songs Without Words*. The *agitato* feeling is achieved not only through the work's fast tempo (two of the *Songs Without Words*, Op. 102, Nos. 1 and 4, are marked *Andante un poco agitato*, reinforcing the assertion attributed to Mendelssohn that *agitato* should not bring about a change in tempo). The sense of excitement and agitation is attained through articulation, dynamics, and touch. The composer's carefully-placed pedal markings accentuate the articulation that generates breathlessness and contributes to the *agitato* feeling.

Two layers of accompaniment—a bass line and broken chords—support a homophonic, chordal, mostly detached melody, further contributing to the feeling of excitement. Be aware, though, that unless carefully shaped and voiced, the repeated chords and back-and-forth motion of the arpeggiated middle layer may create a sense of stepping in place rather than the required forward motion.

Song Without Words in E minor, Op. 62, No 3

Dedicated to his friend Clara Schumann, Op. 62 bears this inscription: *"Frau Dr. Clara Schumann geb. Wieck zugeeignet."*

The title often assigned to this piece, *Trauermarsch*, or Funeral March, may refer to more than just a description of the song's mood. Mendelssohn composed this piece in early 1843; at the time, he may still have been mourning his mother's recent death.[21] The fanfare-like opening, which was not originally part of the composition and only appeared in the first printed edition of this opus, is similar to the opening Gustav Mahler later used in the first movement of his fifth symphony.[22] Short but dramatic, this Song Without Words requires a steady, controlled beat while at the same time respecting the *tranquillo e legato* (m. 5). The *tranquillo* complements the drama of the *f* and *ff* repeated chords, and the legato indicates that the chordal progression, while being vertical and seemingly rhythmic, is first and foremost melodic.

These elements undergo a big transformation in the second half of the piece. The *tranquillo e legato* chords become dramatic and powerful and are now marked **ff** and *con forza*, while the dramatic and forceful chords from the opening become soft and distant, fading into memories and acceptance.

Song Without Words in A Major, Op. 62, No. 6

Dedicated to his friend Clara Schumann, Op. 62 bears this inscription: *"Frau Dr. Clara Schumann geb. Wieck zugeeignet."*

Nicknamed "Spring Song," this is arguably the most charming, graceful, and captivating of the forty-eight *Songs Without Words* and also one of the best known and most beloved. Though pinpointing the source of this piece's charm is perhaps infeasible, some characteristics that make this piece appealing, are worth pointing out. The beautifully shaped melodic line moves in gentle curves and consists of what is possibly a perfect balance between steps and leaps, *staccato* and *legato*, and long and short notes. This line is supported by a delicate, arpeggiated, plucked-like middle layer and by a sparse bass line. The texture is crystal clear, the three layers and numerous notes notwithstanding. The title "Spring Song" befits the song's pleasant, sunny and optimistic disposition. In fact, this composition may reflect Mendelssohn's nature as portrayed by his many friends and acquaintances: friendly, gracious, open, and well mannered (while also serious and strict—above all with himself—when it came to music).

Hans von Bülow uses this work to illustrate what may be the essence of Mendelssohn's music:

> The study of Mendelssohn's piano music will prove more productive for utmost refinement of attack and movement, to the degrees that the limits of purity in his markings are strictly observed; and if it is scarcely possible that a pianist should appear among us who would be capable in the case of the all too well known *Frühlingslied* without Words of producing a showpiece of such grace, unaffected naturalness, and artistic refinement as the master himself in performance, still this study will always lead to a more "musical" music making than tinkling away at Schumann, which significantly encourages melancholy and pathological effusiveness. [23]

Mendelssohn's sparse pedal in the first half of the piece helps maintain the crystalline clarity of the sound and of the plucked-like middle layer. In the second half, however, a longer pedal creates a different color, indicated also by the softer, **pp** dynamics.

Of special note are the double-stemmed notes that serve the dual purpose of melody and accompaniment (for example, E in measures 2, 6, and 10; A in measure 7, etc.). They are marked, simultaneously, as *staccato* and *legato*. The obviously impossible task of following these instructions can be resolved like many other seemingly impossible interpretative challenges, namely, by creating the impression, or illusion, that implies both meanings. For example, the second eighth E in measure 2 should be played *legato* and as an integral part of the top line, but also with an ever so slight accented touch that would be in line with the "plucked" figure of which this E is part. In other words, make sure you have a very clear idea and plan of the various touches and dynamic shades you are going to utilize in this piece. To this end, you should practice and listen to the melody alone, practice and listen to the arpeggiated accompaniment alone (in particular, to the last note of each arpeggio), and do the same for both these lines together. Regarding notes belonging to both melody and accompaniment, see also discussion of Op. 102, No. 4.

Note also that within each measure, the plucked, arpeggiated figure descends, but in the rare cases when it ascends, as in measures 35–42 and 71–77, the second and higher note is accentuated, intensifying the upward motion. The climax of the first of these two ascending lines, in measure 42, further illustrates its expressive quality with the song's only *sforzando* on a non-melody note. (The other *sforzandos*, in measures 12, 16, 18, 29, 33 and 65, are all on downbeats, marking high points in the melody.)

Song Without Words in B-flat Major, Op. 67, No 3

The first two beats of this Song Without Words have no harmony, only a melody and its syncopated echo, or reflection, an octave below. While the syncopated element persists throughout the piece all the way to the very last note, at times it imitates the melodic line (mm. 8–9, 26–27, 46–47) and other times its function is rhythmic (mm. 2–4, 6–8, 19–26, 28–30, etc.).

It is vital to feel and play the composition in two beats, applying the *andante tranquillo* to the quarter note, not the eighth. Likewise, it is important to have a clear sense of the downbeat and to note how the up- and downbeats are often at odds with the melody's contour. For example, the first statement of the melody starts on a high note upbeat and descends towards the downbeat (m. 1). It then rises again, once again reaching the highest point on the weak beat (m. 3, second beat). Likewise, the dynamics in measures 3 and 29, and the **sf** in measure 22, emphasize the weak beats. Adding to the intricacies, Mendelssohn does not consistently stress the weak-beat. In measures 32, 36–37, 39, and 46 he very clearly places **_sf_** signs on the strong beat. These details may at first seem somewhat confusing but they, in fact, lend the piece flexibility against the backdrop of persistent, consistent syncopations that add an underlying intensity.

See also Op. 85, No. 2 for a discussion on how similar means can accomplish rather different ends.

Song Without Words in A minor, Op. 85, No. 2

Op. 85 and Op. 102 were compiled and published posthumously by Simrock, who was eager to keep publishing these highly popular titles.

The *agitato* indication should not be mistaken to mean a faster tempo (Mendelssohn was "annoyed when his *agitato* was misinterpreted as a tempo change"[24]). The tempo is allegro; *agitato* is the qualifier that refers to the mood, the spirit of the piece. What are the elements and details of this song that create the agitato character? Articulation, in and of itself, can help, but is especially effective when occurring between a short note and a longer one that follows, as is the case throughout this piece. Also, the highest pitches of the melody do not occur on the downbeat but rather on the third and weaker beat. This tension between the first beat's inherent stress and the curve of the musical line—often accentuated by a mid-measure *sforzando* (mm. 6, 13, 18, etc.)—enhances the *agitato* feeling. In addition, the middle voice keeps the piece moving even during the melody's longer-value notes.

Make sure that the upbeat at the start of the piece does not sound like a downbeat. Note the different slurs for similar passages: compare, for example, measures 1–3 to measures 5–7. Also note that in the second half of the piece the **_sf_**'s no longer occur on the third beat as in measures 6, 13, 16, 18 and 20 but rather on the downbeat (mm. 33 and 34). The song ends on a weak beat, bringing this *agitato* piece to a pianissimo ending on a "feminine" cadence.

It is interesting to compare this Song Without Words to the one just preceding it in this collection, Op. 67, No. 3 in B-flat Major. They are very different from one another. Most obvious is, of course, the fact that one is an *Andante tranquillo* while the other an *Allegro agitato*. The texture, too, is different: one contains an abundance of chords, the other doesn't. Yet these different results are achieved through various similar means: voices echoing or imitating one another and discord between metric stresses and melodic contours. Both also start on upbeats but end with full measures.

Song Without Words in C Major, Op. 102, No. 3

Like Op. 85, Op. 102 was also compiled and published posthumously by Simrock under the highly popular title *Songs Without Words*.

One of Mendelssohn's most original, imaginative and characteristic musical effects was the scherzo-like genre that consists of short, staccato, fast, light, often high-pitched notes that can clearly depict fleeting, fairy-like characters. The Rondo Capriccioso in E Major, Op. 14 and the Scherzo in E minor, Op. 16 are typical example of this style. In orchestral music this is well represented by the violins' part at the beginning and in the scherzo of the Overture to *A Midsummer Night's Dream*, Op. 21.

Marked *presto* and *staccato* throughout (as the staccato in the first two and last few measures seems to imply), this Song Without Words is closely related to the style mentioned above, although it does not make extensive use of the high register. Still, the study of this work offers a taste of some of Mendelssohn's most distinctive musical and technical traits.

Entitled *Kinderstück* (Children's Piece), it isn't an easy piece by any means. Playing constant, *presto*, *staccato* notes, especially when combined with chords, can be hard. The Schirmer Library of Musical Classics 1915 edition of this Song Without Words is similar to the Breitkopf and Härtel Complete Edition, published between 1874 and 1877, which in turn seems similar to the English and German First Editions. In these editions, some notes in both the right and the left hand are missing, making the piece technically easier to play. Measure 63 is omitted entirely.

Schirmer's Library of Musical Classics, 1915
Op. 102, No. 3, mm. 50—64

Song Without Words in G minor, Op. 102, No. 4

The *un poco agitato* in this captivating Song Without Words refers to the mood and character of the piece, not the tempo, which is *andante*. (See also Op. 85 No. 2 in A Minor, above, for a comment on *agitato* in Mendelssohn). *Un poco agitato* indicates that the piece is not unreservedly tranquil. Uncharacteristically, this song consists of only two layers: an expressive, poignant melody and an accompaniment that surges and swells in large curves. These swells create an undercurrent of agitation apparent already in the first half of the piece, which is otherwise free of any drama. There are two curves, or waves per measure, each starting low and rising two to three octaves (mm. 6, 11, 27, etc.), sometimes merging briefly with the melodic line but never crossing it, always staying beneath it. The one exception occurs in measure 20 where the melody comes to a stop, allowing the accompaniment to take over, rising high, and gradually transitioning in measure 22 into a "rebirth" of the melodic line.

There are many different ways in which to finger this piece. Personally, I do not think that the hands must necessarily be divided according to how the notes appear on the two staves. Instead, the focus should be on fingering that nicely shapes the melody, allowing it to sing, while making the accompaniment sound as if it is played by a single hand. Feel free to find the fingering and hand distribution that work best for you—and for the music.

Song Without Words in C Major, Op. 102, No. 6

The last of the forty-eight Songs Without Words, this is one of the easiest, most straightforward, and uncomplicated songs. Written in C Major and being mostly homophonic with relatively simple rhythms (quarter notes, eights, and dotted notes) and moving in an *andante* pace, it sounds clean and innocent.

That said, we must remember that achieving a performance that sounds pure, unspoiled, and simple isn't simple at all. The tempo should be steady and flowing but neither rushed nor dragging; the dynamics should be strictly observed but never extreme, never exceeding the *p-f* range; articulation signs and the various touches—*legato, portato, staccato*—should be carefully observed; lines, whether *legato* or *staccato*, whether consisting of single notes or of chords, should be clearly shaped. And finally, the tone has to sing and the chords be carefully voiced.

This is an excellent piece for students to study as soon as their hands are large enough to play the chords and the octaves. The sensitive among them can quite easily executed the pure simplicity of this piece but even those less-sensitive can enjoy it and greatly benefit from it.

—Immanuela Gruenberg

Notes

1 Letter to Souchay, 15 October 1842, quoted by Botstein, Leon. "The aesthetics of Assimilation and Affirmation: Reconstructing the Career of Felix Mendelssohn" in *Mendelssohn and his World*, ed. R. Larry Todd. (Princeton: Princeton University Press, 1991), 31.

2 Sternberg, Constantin von, ed. *Mendelssohn: Songs Without Words for the Piano*. (New York: G. Schirmer, Inc., 1915).

3 Pfeiffer, Theodor. *The Piano Master Classes of Hans von Bülow: Two Participants' Accounts*. Richard Louis Zimdars, trans. (Bloomington and Indianapolis: Indiana University Press, 1993), 61.

4 Elvers, Rudolph. *Felix Mendelssohn: A Life in Letters*. Craig Tomlinson, trans. (New York: Fromm International Publishing Corporation, 1986).

5 Hamilton, Kenneth. "Mendelssohn and the Piano" in *Mendelssohn in Performance*, Siegwart Reichwald, ed. (Bloomington and Indianapolis: Indiana University Press, 2008).

6 quoted in *Mendelssohn and his World*, ed. R. Larry Todd. (Princeton: Princeton University Press, 1991), 241.

7 Lampadius, W.A.. *Life of Felix Mendelssohn Bartholdy*, trans. W. L. Gage, quoted in R. Larry Todd. "Piano Music Reformed: The Case of Felix Mendelssohn Bartholdy" in *Nineteenth Century Piano Music*, R. Larry Todd, ed. 178–179.

8 Todd, R. Larry. "Mendelssohn, Felix: Early Years." *Grove Music Online*, www.grovemusic.com (accessed 25 December, 2013).

9 Todd, R. Larry. "Mendelssohn, Felix: Apprenticeship and early maturity, 1821–9." *Grove Music Online*, www.grovemusic.com (accessed 25 December, 2013).

10 Hamilton, Kenneth. "Mendelssohn and the Piano" in *Mendelssohn in Performance*, Siegwart Reichwald, ed. (Bloomington and Indianapolis: Indiana University Press, 2008), 23.

11 Todd, R. Larry. "Piano Music Reformed: The Case of Felix Mendelssohn Bartholdy" in *Nineteenth Century Piano Music*, R. Larry Todd, ed. 178.

12 Pfeiffer, Theodor. *The Piano Master Classes of Hans von Bülow: Two Participants' Accounts*. Richard Louis Zimdars, trans. (Bloomington and Indianapolis: Indiana University Press, 1993), 61.

13 Ibid., 23–25.

14 Ibid., 31.

15 Ibid., 31.

16 Grove, Sir George, "Mendelssohn," in *Dictionary of Music and Musicians*, ed. Sir George Grove (London: Macmillan, 1880), 2:298, quoted in Hamilton, Kenneth. *Mendelssohn and the Piano*.

17 *Philadelphia National Gazette*, 20 August 1841, quoted in Hamilton, Kenneth. *Mendelssohn and the Piano*.

18 Little, William. "Mendelssohn and Liszt," in *Mendelssohn Studies*, ed. Larry Todd (Cambridge: Cambridge University Press, 1992), 118.

19 Pfeiffer, Theodor. *The Piano Master Classes of Hans von Bülow: Two Participants' Accounts*. Richard Louis Zimdars, trans. (Bloomington and Indianapolis: Indiana University Press, 1993), 85.

20 Todd, R. Larry, ed. *Mendelssohn Bartholdy: Lieder ohne Worte*. Kassel: Bärenreiter, 2009, p. 191.

21 Ibid, p. IV.

22 Ibid.

23 Hans von Bülow. *Briefe und Schriften. Bd 3. Ausgewahlte Schriften: 1850–1892*. (Leipzig: Breikopf & Härtel, 1896), p. 209; trans, by Susan Gillespie in *Mendelssohn and His World*, ed. R Larry Todd (Princeton: Princeton University Press, 1991), p. 393.

24 Hogwood, Christopher. "Foreword" to *Mendelssohn in Performance*, ed. Siegwart Reichwald (Bloomington: Indiana University Press, 2008), ix.

Song Without Words in A minor

Felix Mendelssohn
Op. 19b, No. 2

Andante espressivo

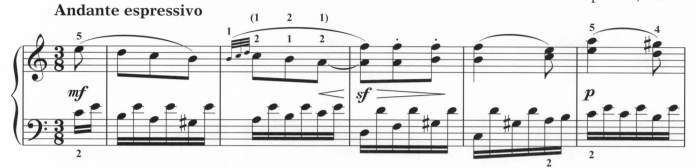

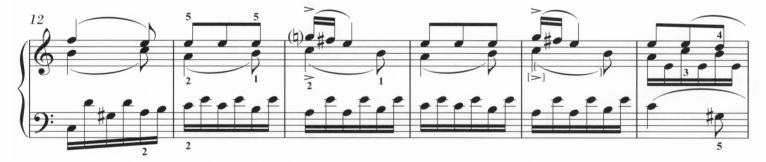

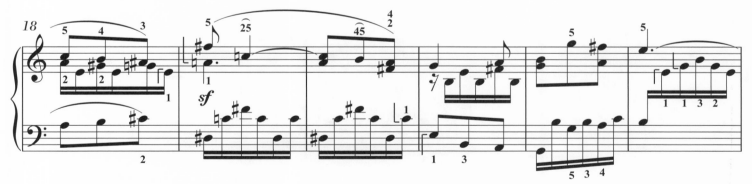

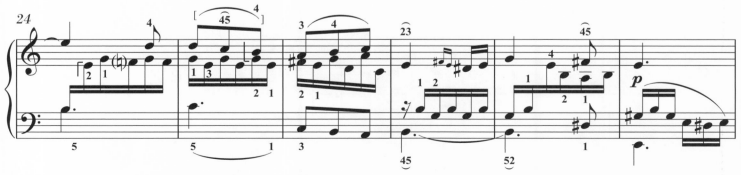

Copyright © 2014 by G. Schirmer, Inc. (ASCAP) New York, NY
International Copyright Secured.   All Rights Reserved.

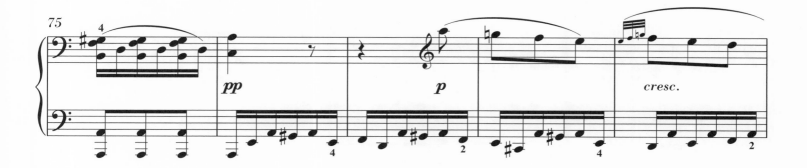

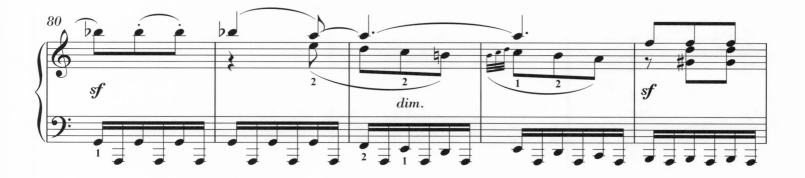

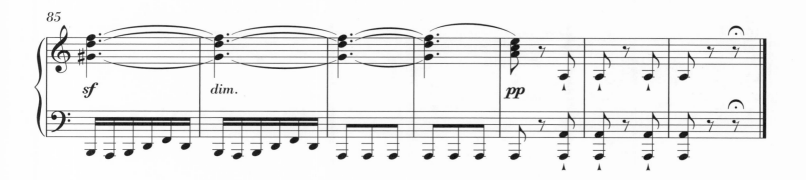

Song Without Words A Major

Felix Mendelssohn
Op. 19b, No. 3

Molto Allegro e vivace

Copyright © 2014 by G. Schirmer, Inc. (ASCAP) New York, NY
International Copyright Secured. All Rights Reserved.

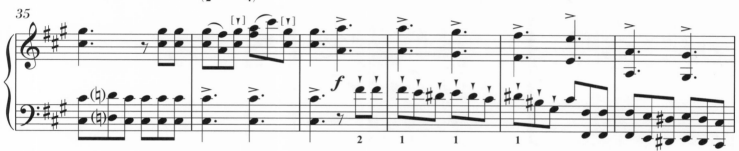

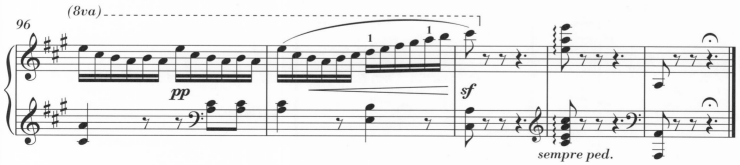

Song Without Words in G minor
"Venetian Gondola Song"

Felix Mendelssohn
Op. 19b, No. 6

Andante sostenuto

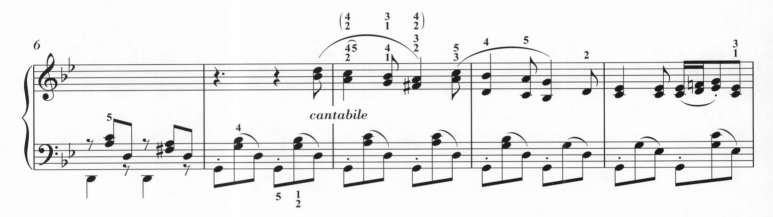

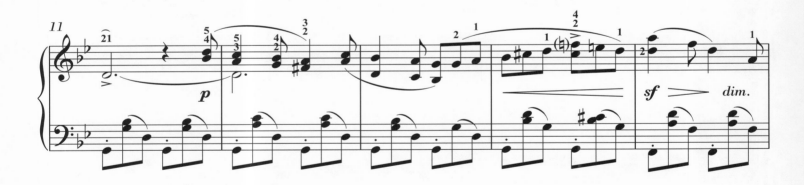

Copyright © 2014 by G. Schirmer, Inc. (ASCAP) New York, NY
International Copyright Secured.   All Rights Reserved.

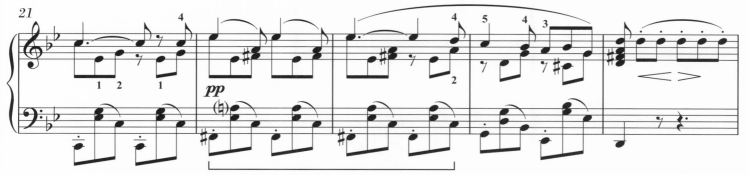

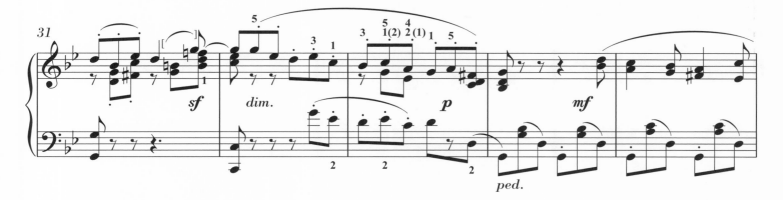

Song Without Words in E Major

Felix Mendelssohn
Op. 30, No. 3

Adagio non troppo

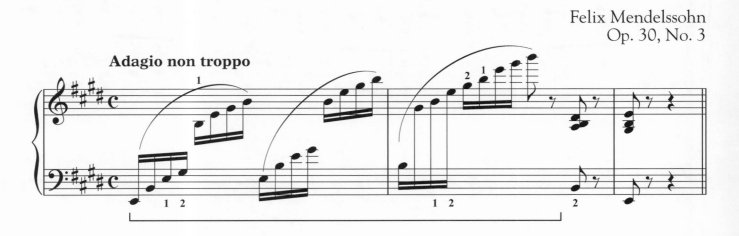

Copyright © 2014 by G. Schirmer, Inc. (ASCAP) New York, NY
International Copyright Secured.   All Rights Reserved.

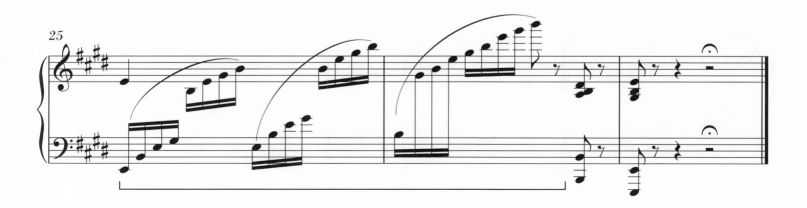

Song Without Words in F-sharp minor
"Venetian Gondola Song"

Felix Mendelssohn
Op. 30, No. 6

Allegretto tranquillo

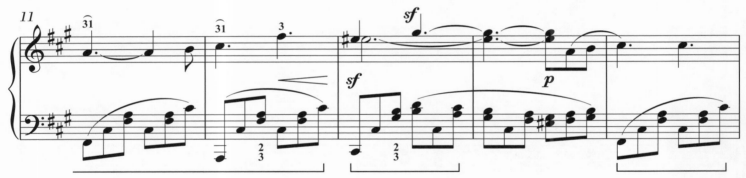

Copyright © 2014 by G. Schirmer, Inc. (ASCAP) New York, NY
International Copyright Secured.   All Rights Reserved.

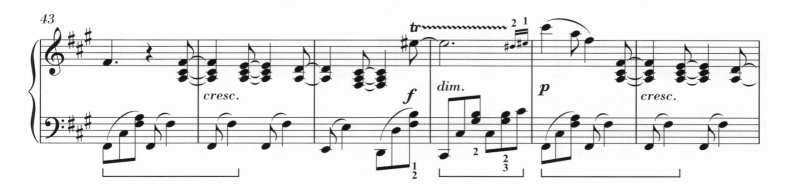

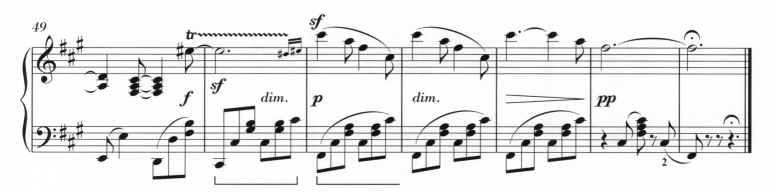

Song Without Words in A-flat Major

"Duet"

N.B.: The two voices must always be emphasized very clearly

Felix Mendelssohn
Op. 38, No. 6

Andante con moto

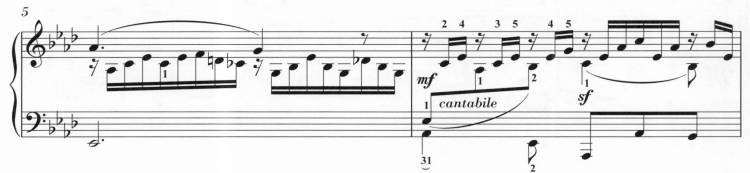

Copyright © 2014 by G. Schirmer, Inc. (ASCAP) New York, NY
International Copyright Secured.   All Rights Reserved.

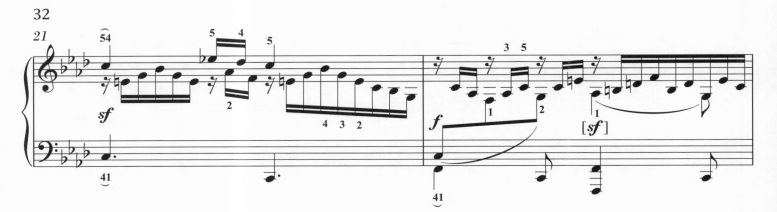

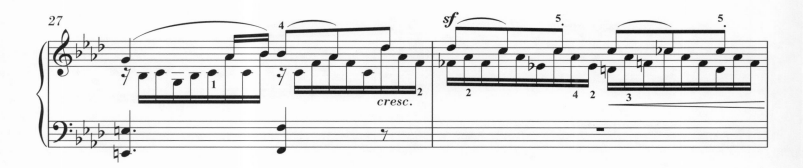

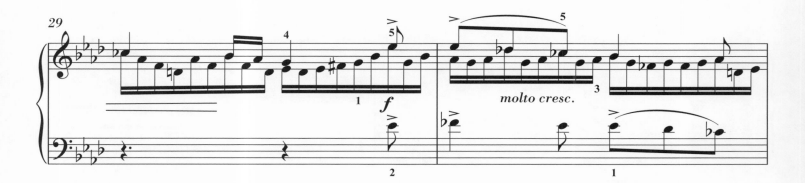

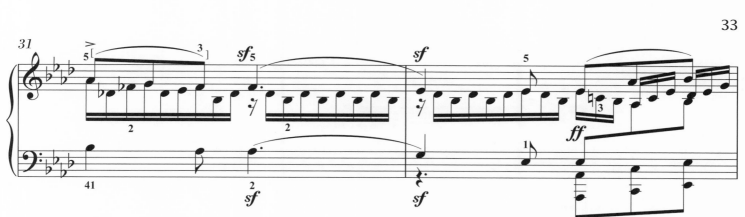

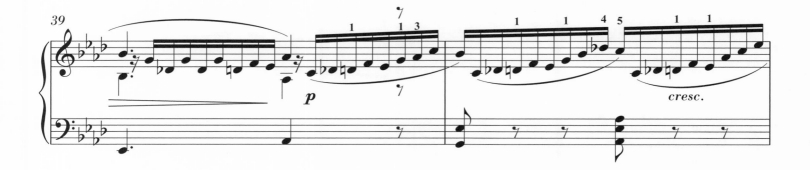

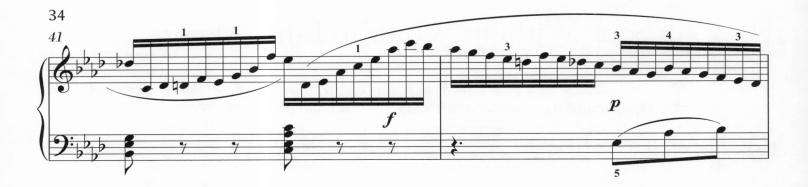

Song Without Words in E-flat Major

Felix Mendelssohn
Op. 53, No. 2

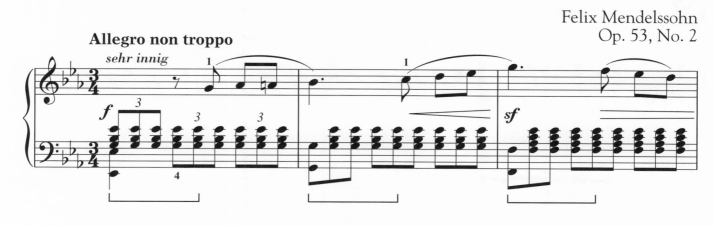

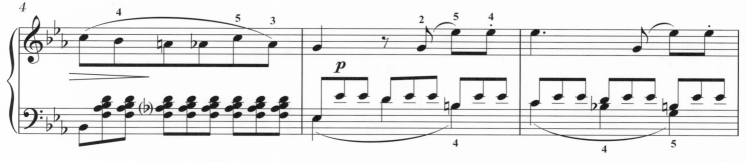

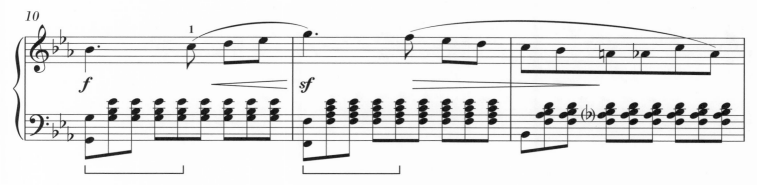

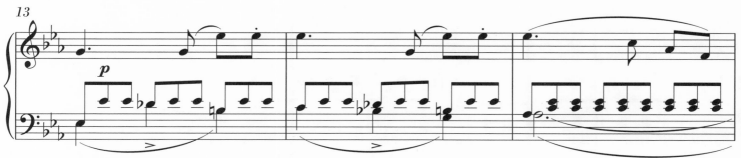

Copyright © 2014 by G. Schirmer, Inc. (ASCAP) New York, NY
International Copyright Secured.   All Rights Reserved.

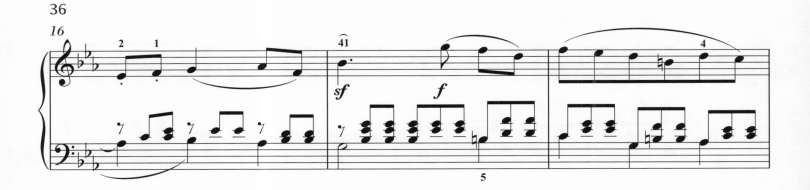

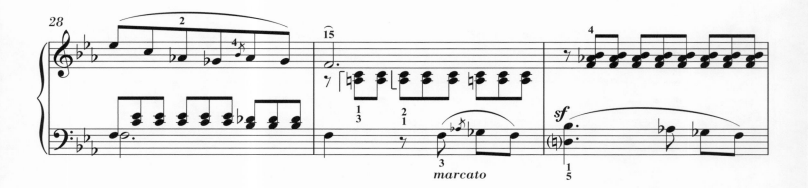

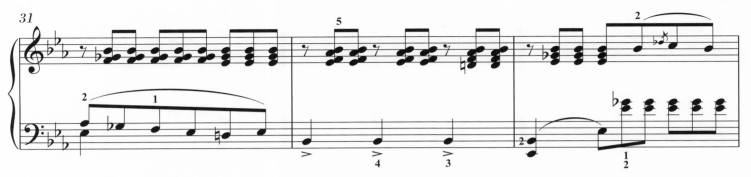

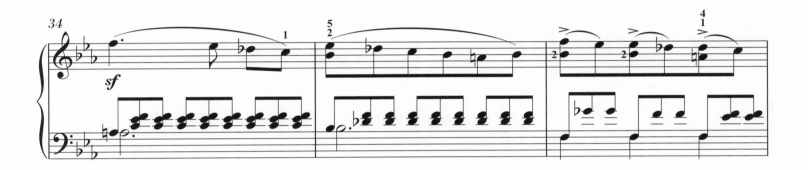

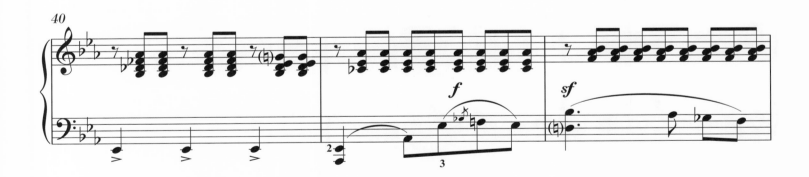

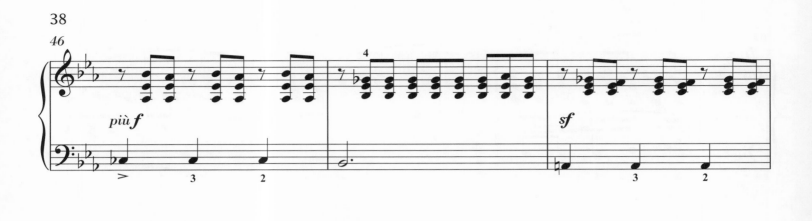

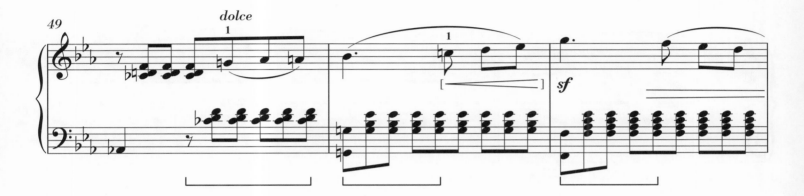

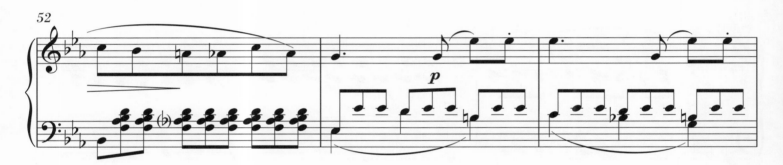

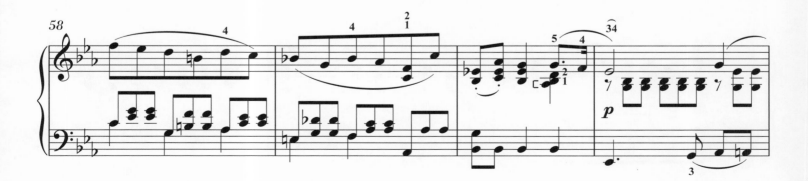

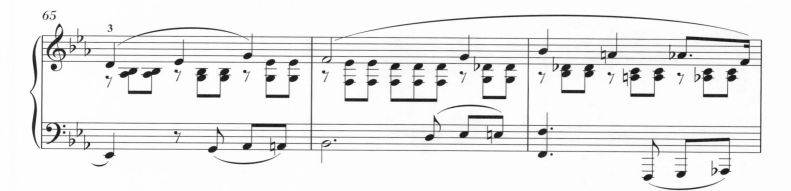

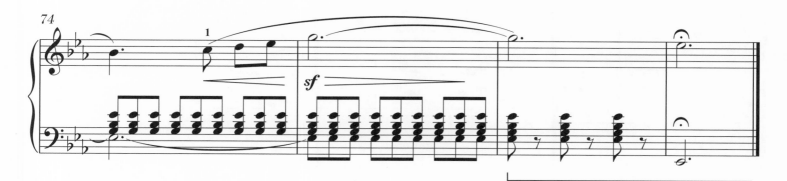

Song Without Words in G minor

Felix Mendelssohn
Op. 53, No. 3

Copyright © 2014 by G. Schirmer, Inc. (ASCAP) New York, NY
International Copyright Secured.   All Rights Reserved.

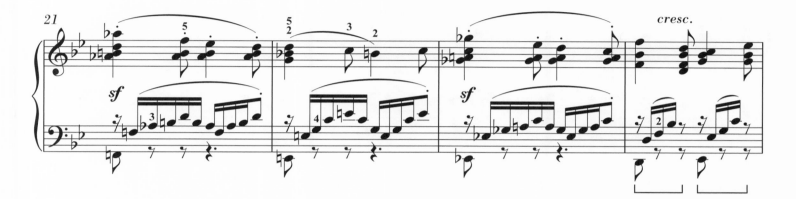

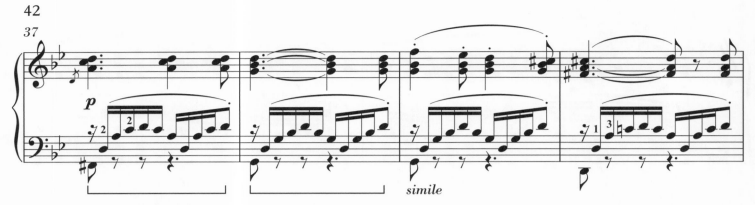

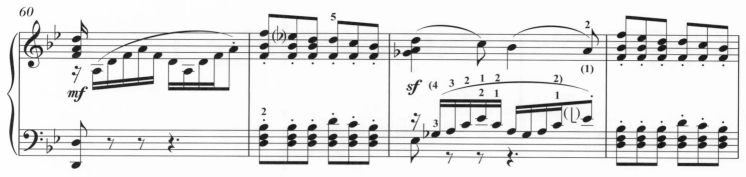

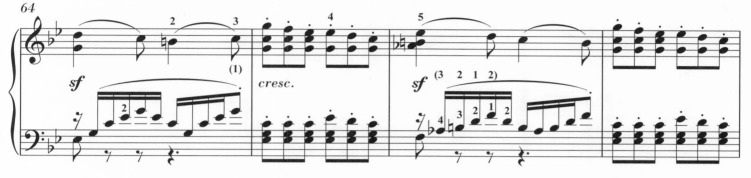

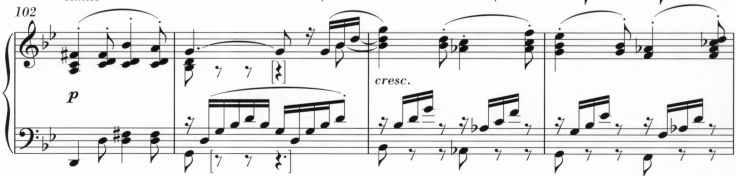

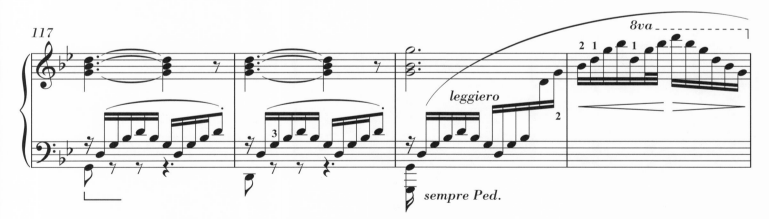

Song Without Words in E minor

Felix Mendelssohn
Op. 62, No. 3

Andante maestoso

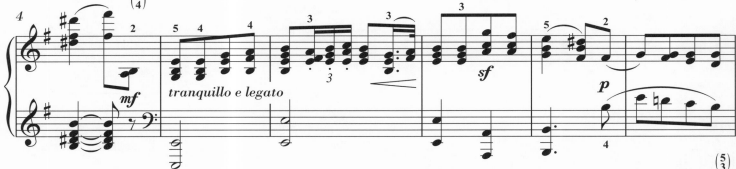

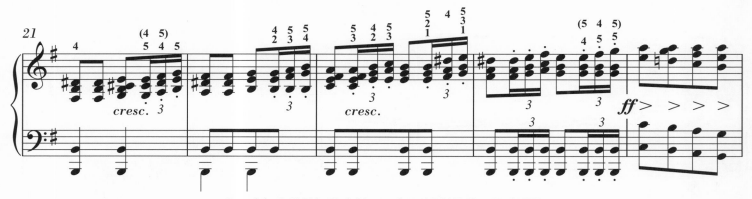

Copyright © 2014 by G. Schirmer, Inc. (ASCAP) New York, NY
International Copyright Secured.   All Rights Reserved.

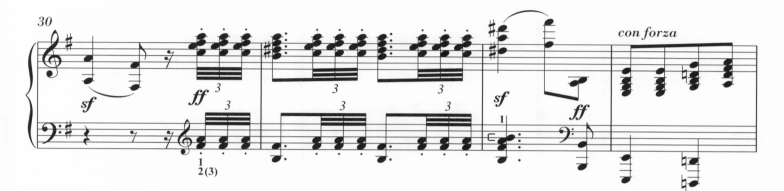

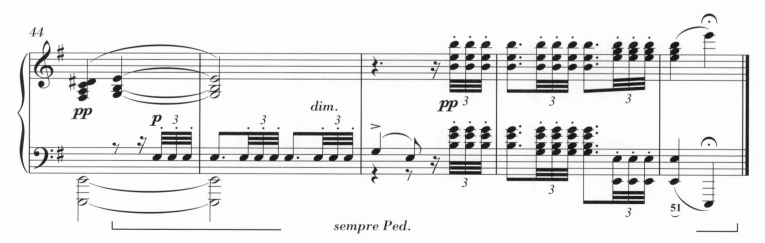

Song Without Words in A Major

Felix Mendelssohn
Op. 62, No. 6

Allegretto grazioso

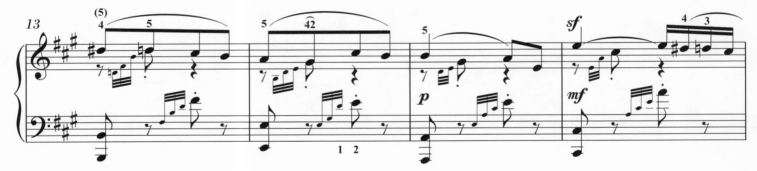

Copyright © 2014 by G. Schirmer, Inc. (ASCAP) New York, NY
International Copyright Secured.   All Rights Reserved.

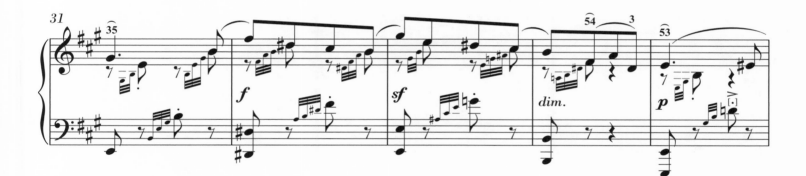

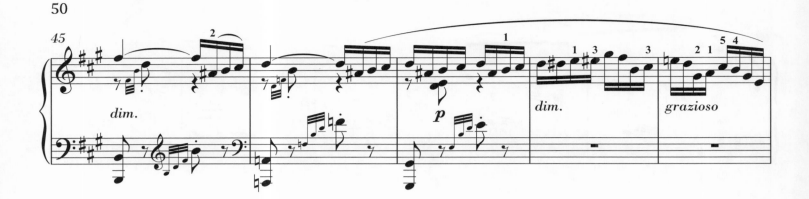

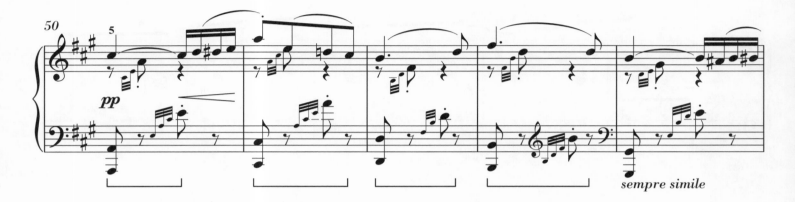

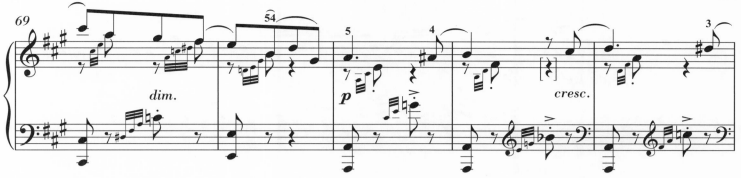

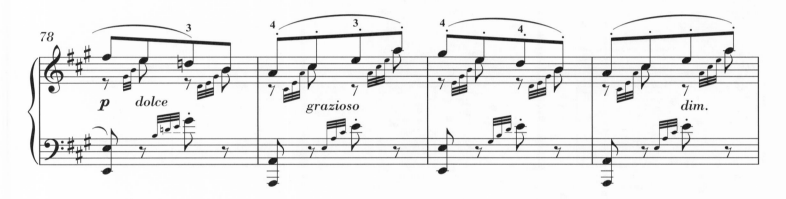

Song Without Words in B-flat Major

Felix Mendelssohn
Op. 67, No. 3

Andante tranquillo

Copyright © 2014 by G. Schirmer, Inc. (ASCAP) New York, NY
International Copyright Secured.   All Rights Reserved.

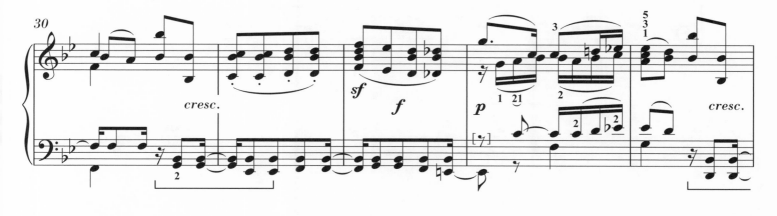

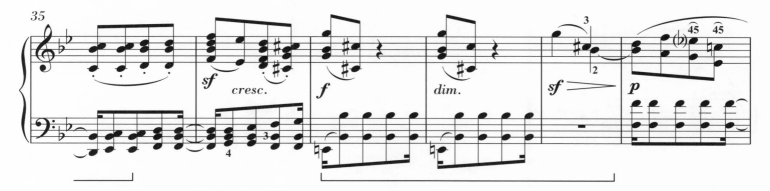

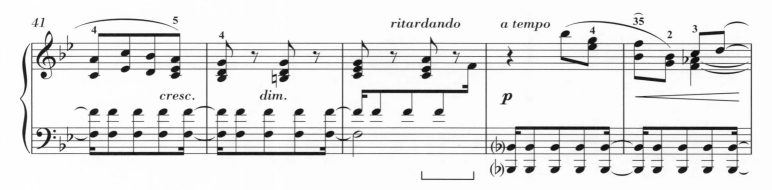

Song Without Words in A minor

Felix Mendelssohn
Op. 85, No. 2

Allegro agitato

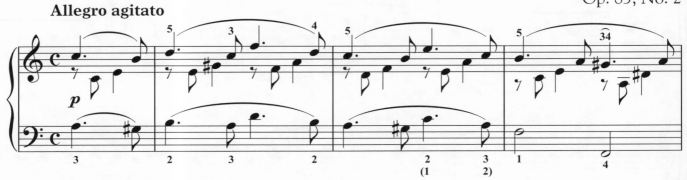

Copyright © 2014 by G. Schirmer, Inc. (ASCAP) New York, NY
International Copyright Secured.   All Rights Reserved.

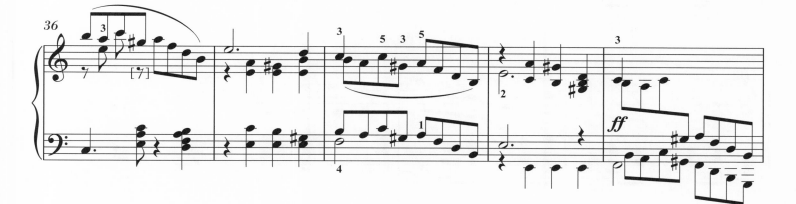

*Left hand, finger 5 substitutes right hand, finger 3.

Song Without Words in C Major

Felix Mendelssohn
Op. 102, No. 3

Copyright © 2014 by G. Schirmer, Inc. (ASCAP) New York, NY
International Copyright Secured.   All Rights Reserved.

*LH plays G2 and F3; RH plays G3, B3, and D4.

Song Without Words in G minor

Felix Mendelssohn
Op. 102, No. 4

Andante un poco agitato

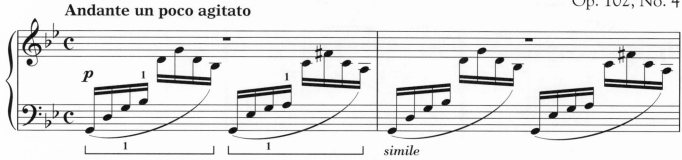

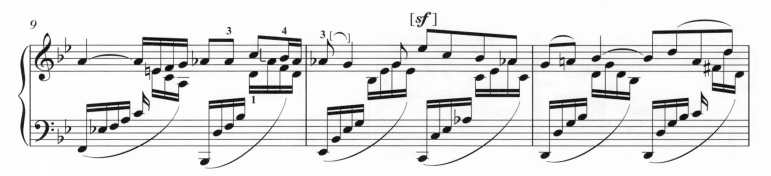

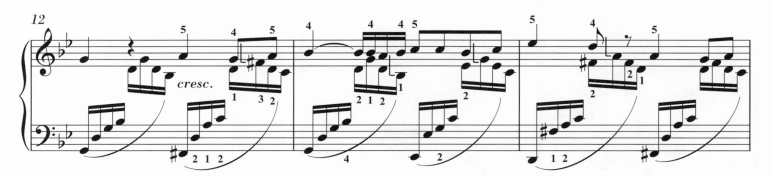

Copyright © 2014 by G. Schirmer, Inc. (ASCAP) New York, NY
International Copyright Secured.   All Rights Reserved.

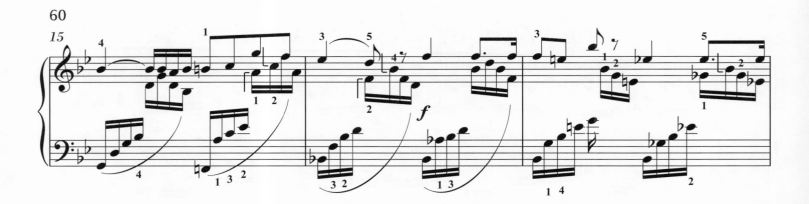

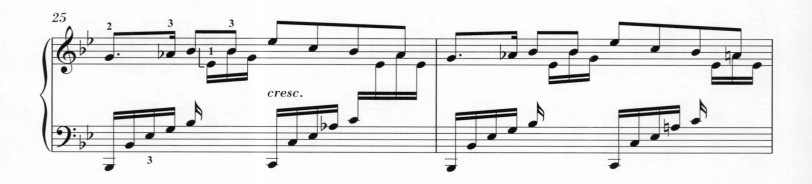

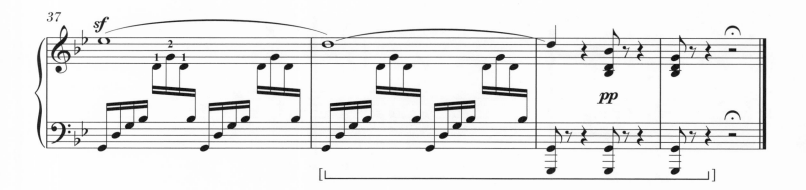

Song Without Words in C Major

Felix Mendelssohn
Op. 102, No. 6

Copyright © 2014 by G. Schirmer, Inc. (ASCAP) New York, NY
International Copyright Secured.   All Rights Reserved.

ABOUT THE EDITOR

IMMANUELA GRUENBERG

Active as a recitalist, chamber pianist, teacher and clinician, Immanuela Gruenberg has appeared in the United States, South America, Israel, and the Far East. She has presented workshops, master classes and lectures on piano performance, piano literature and pedagogy. Critics have praised her playing as "supreme artistry" (*Richmond News Leader*), "lyrical and dramatic" (*Buenos Aires Herald*) and noted her "delicate sonorities" (*Haaretz*, Israel). She was lauded for her "highly intelligent" writing, "scholarly" and "well thought out" research, for lectures that "exceeded our highest expectations," for programs of "unusual interest" and for having "spoke[n] intelligently about each piece" (*The Washington Post*).

She began her musical career in Israel, performing as soloist and as member of the Tel Aviv Trio in venues that include the Chamber Music Series of the Israel Philharmonic Orchestra, the Israel Museum in Jerusalem and the Tel Aviv Museum of Art. She appeared on Buenos Aires Classical Radio, and recorded for Israel's Classical Radio where she was featured repeatedly. In the United States she appeared on stages such as the Kennedy Center for the Performing Arts, the Corcoran Gallery, the Strathmore Mansion and the Smithsonian's "Piano 300" series, celebrating the 300th anniversary of the invention of the piano. Other "anniversary" performances include lecture recitals in Israel and the United States on Schubert's posthumously-published sonatas—the topic of her doctoral dissertation—in honor of the composer's bicentennial anniversary and a performance of Josef Tal's Concerto for Piano and Electronics in honor of the composer's 85th birthday. She presented lectures and clinics at colleges and universities, for various

MTA chapters, at conventions, at the World Piano Pedagogy Conference, the National Conference on Keyboard Pedagogy, as well as for the general public. Dr. Gruenberg taught master classes at the Central Conservatory of Music in Beijing, China, the Liszt Academy in Buenos Aires, for the Latin American Association of Pianists and Pedagogue, and in various venues in the US and Israel. A much sought after adjudicator, Immanuela Gruenberg also served as chair of the Washington International Competition. She currently serves on the editorial committee of American Music Teacher, the official publication of Music Teachers National Association, on the National Conference on Keyboard Pedagogy's Committee on Independent Music Teachers, and is Vice President for Programs for Montgomery County, MD, MTA.

A magna cum laude graduate of the Rubin Academy of Music of the Tel Aviv University and a thirteen-time winner of the America Israel Cultural Foundation scholarships, Dr. Gruenberg is the recipient of numerous prizes and awards. As a scholarship student at the Manhattan School of Music she completed the Doctor of Musical Arts program in only two years. She studied piano with Arie Vardi (for over ten years) and Constance Keene and chamber music with Boris Berman and Rami Shevelov. She also coached with Pnina Salzman and Thomas Schumacher.

A teacher of award winning students, Dr. Gruenberg was a teaching assistant at the Manhattan School of Music in New York, a faculty member of the Music Teachers' College in Tel Aviv and the Levine School of Music in Washington, DC, and maintains an independent studio in Potomac, Maryland.